Laura Franck KCC £2.99

..19

G000113018

THINK DOG

RULES FOR LIFE

HOW TO GET THE BEST OUT OF LIFE AND PEOPLE

Will and Annalese Murray
and Dog!

Friendly
Publishing
Ltd

To George and Henry

We love you so much!
Lead by example
Encourage others
Think Dog
Be loyal to those you love

Many thanks – Richard Burton, Tom and the team at Sparks, our
families and friends who have kept us on the straight and narrow!

First published in 2005 by
Friendly Publishing Ltd
PO Box 192
Evesham
Worcestershire WR11 7WW
UK
www.friendlypublishing.com

Copyright © 2005 Will and Annalese Murray.

All Rights Reserved. No part of this publication may be reproduced, stored in a
retrieval system or transmitted in any form or by any means, electronic, mechani-
cal, photocopying, recording, scanning or otherwise, except under the terms of
the Copyright Licensing Agency Ltd, 90 Tottenham Court Road, London, W1P 0LP,
UK, without the permission in writing of the Publisher.

Will and Annalese Murray have asserted their right under the Copyright, Designs
and Patents Act 1988, to be identified as the authors and illustrators of this work.

ISBN 0-9550897-0-0

Text design and typesetting by Sparks – www.sparks.co.uk
Cover design by Murray Murray – www.murraymurray.com

Printed and bound in Great Britain by Cambrian Printers Ltd, Aberystwyth

THE THINK DOG TALE

WELCOME TO THINK DOG

From Will and Annalese Murray

For many years now we have been helping people develop better relationships at work (a huge task by anyone's standards!) so watching 'Dog' skip effortlessly past problems that trouble the rest of us on a daily basis has been a truly awesome learning experience.

In our opinion 'Dog' is the world's best relationship and life coach, not because he talks a good game, but because the things he does on a daily basis flow naturally from his desire to please others whilst also getting the most out of life himself.

'DOG' RELIES SOLELY ON HIS RELATIONSHIPS TO SURVIVE

Without his wonderful relationships 'Dog' wouldn't eat, find shelter or have much fun at all, but through building strong, loving, fair, two-way relationships with both humans and other dogs he gets everything he needs to live a cool, satisfying life.

Doesn't sound bad, does it?

'DOG' EMBRACES LIFE WHOLEHEARTEDLY

'Dog' gives 100% to everything he does. He thinks that if something is worth doing it's worth doing well – he doesn't do half measures.

'DOG' IS TOUGH AND COURAGEOUS

Dog never looks for trouble but if trouble comes looking for him then he doesn't run away either. When you need a friend, look no further.

'DOG' OWNS NOTHING

You don't see 'Dog' fussing about the latest craze or how much stuff he's got back at his kennel. 'Dog' travels light; he's never weighed down by excess baggage and never tries to keep up with the Mutleys down the road. Whatever he needs people share with him, because they love him for who he is.

'DOG' GIVES FREELY

Despite having no real possessions 'Dog' shares the things he does have without thinking – his love, his time and himself. In fact, 'Dog' is amazingly generous and giving to everyone he meets.

'DOG' IS COMPLETELY LOYAL

Dog never lets his friends down. That's not to say that he doesn't make a few mistakes or annoy everyone from time to time, but he has the kindest, most genuine heart in the world and would do anything for those he loves.

Which makes a few mistakes pretty forgivable.

'DOG' IS IRRESISTIBLE

It's not just because he looks gorgeous either.

When 'Dog' focuses those big eyes on you and gives you 100% of his attention he is truly irresistible. He has mastered the knack of making you feel that you are the most important person in his life; whether you actually are or whether you just happen to be holding a chocolate biscuit.

'DOG' IS LOVED FOR WHO HE IS

'Dog' comes without airs and graces or pretensions. With 'Dog', what you see is what you get. That is what makes him so special – he doesn't have to try to be something he's not because everyone loves him for being utterly genuine.

> Proven over thousands of years of doggy desirability the Think Dog Rules will help you:

GET MORE OUT OF LIFE AND LOVE

Think Dog will help you enjoy everything good that life has to offer.

You can transform yourself into an opportunity magnet and – who knows? – your new found good fortune might extend to your love life too. Look at 'Dog' – he is a real 'hotdog' when it comes to the ladies!

BECOME MORE POPULAR AND SELF CONFIDENT

Think Dog is a surefire way to become more popular and with growing popularity comes greater self confidence.

These 'Rules for Life' really work … guaranteed.

RESPOND POSITIVELY TO ALL KINDS OF BULLYING

Thinking 'Dog' will make you a less obvious target for bullies and help you to respond successfully to bullying behaviour.

If you are secretly scared that you have the potential to be a bully yourself, the rules will stop you before you even go there.

MAKE A BIGGER DIFFERENCE

Life is for living, loving and sharing, and *Think Dog* will help you do all three.

We **ALL** have the capacity to do amazing things, but some get on and do them whilst others just sit by and watch. Use the rules and become a 'doer'.

BECOME MUCH HAPPIER

No dog or man can be truly happy as an island, so start to 'Think Dog' and build a bridge to those you want to share your life with.

IMPROVE EVERY ASPECT OF YOUR LIFE

Think Dog will change you from the inside out. These rules will help you to see what is life changing and what is life wasting!

CHANGE YOUR LIFE FOREVER

You will never look back once you have started *Think Dog*. These rules are exactly what they say they are: rules for life and not just for Christmas.

> Good luck everyone and we hope you get as much out of reading and applying the Think Dog Rules for Life as we have done from helping 'Dog' to write them!
>
> Will and Annalese
> XXXXX

A DOG'S EYE VIEW

You may have heard it from the horse's mouth before but now you can enjoy the real thing: a dog's eye view.

Living with humans I have observed that what you seem to want more than anything are some good friends you can rely on.

Fair enough, I say; to a dog this is like falling off a log or chasing a stick. We learn this stuff at puppy preschool. Every time I go to the park I make new friends – dogs and humans alike. Grandmas want to pet me, kids want to stroke me and cute lady dogs go wild just for a sniff of me.

So why do you humans take a simple thing like being everyone's best friend and make it so hard?

It's been troubling us dogs for years. In fact it was seeing good humans suffer that has made me take the plunge and share my amazing secrets of doggy desirability with you, the human race.

Taking matters into my own paws I have created the Think Dog Rules for Life. These are the secrets that doggy mums and dads have passed on by word of mouth to countless generations of eager young pups. In fact this stuff is so special and so secret that it has never been written down before – until now.

Making friends and sharing your life harmoniously with other people is one of the most rewarding things in the world for both dogs and humans alike. We all enjoy being popular and having fun, but for many people this is far easier said than done.

Don't despair though, because this is exactly what I can teach you.

ME AND MY HUMAN PETS

'What do you know about the trials and tribulations of being a human?', I hear you ask.

Well, let me start by telling you a bit about myself and some of the humans that I have come to love.

For what it's worth, my human name is Ludwig but my friends call me 'Dog'. I am a mix of several different doggy breeds with major chunks of Doberman and Weimaraner.

You might refer to me as a mongrel, which is exactly why you need my help. Think about it for a moment: no dog, however mixed up, likes being called a mongrel!

Looking after George, my human pet, has been a real eye opener. How can an intelligent human being make so many basic mistakes before finishing breakfast? I have listened and learned from George's attempts to steer Henry into the world of tidy bedrooms but regularly had to ask myself why he repeatedly let his passion and belief drive him to lock horns with his work colleagues … occasionally with disastrous results.

Not that it ever stopped me loving him.

Then there is George's wife, Hannah. She's a real sweetie but could be getting so much more out of her life and relationships if she knew how.

Why does she so often side step the big issues at work in order to keep the peace, and at home why does she always get it wrong when trying to give Grace the benefit of her experience – like when she shares her honest opinion on Grace's latest boyfriend?

I also look after the two supposed little ones: Grace, 17, cute and sassy but full of angst, and Henry, 9, with more savvy than the rest of them put together. Maybe he was a dog in a previous life.

Watching Grace I have learned all about the trials and tribulations of college life and growing personal independence.

I have suffered anxious days observing her dive into the ever-buzzing world of college politics, nights out with friends and, last but not least, getting to grips (quite literally sometimes) with boys: and had to be there at the end of the night to pick up the highly emotional pieces.

I have marvelled at Henry's attempts to become master of the playground and sat back in admiration as he's wrapped teachers around his little finger or persuaded Grandma and Grandad to back his latest scam.

Looking after my pets has taught me a lot. They are all wonderful people in a human sort of way, but I have often wondered what they could achieve if only they had a wise old doggy head on their shoulders.

My doggy friends and I began to recognise the opportunity. We knew that some of our innate doggy relationship skills could be transferred between species because of what we had been able to teach Puffball and Alexis who, despite being cats, are now really good friends of ours. (But please don't broadcast it!)

If we could help a couple of cats to think a bit more like us then surely we should be able to help our humans to think a bit like us as well.

This is why, on behalf of all my chums, I have taken on the responsibility of sharing our canine Rules for Life with you, the human race.

WHY ME?

Why am I 'Man's Best Friend' and why do I think I can help you?

My doggy relationship skills have made me the dog I am today to the point that I rely solely on these skills to live.

It is a bit frightening to think that without these relationship and life skills I would be even less use than a cat. (Only joking, Puffball!)

I own nothing – not even the collar I stand up in; I have no wealth, no possessions, but everything I need to live is given to me freely by my pets.

I have learnt the importance of loyalty and try to be loyal to those I love at all times.

I greet my pets when they come home, listen to them and love them unconditionally.

I watch out for my doggy friends like Genghis and Nora, and always try to be there when they need me.

I am certainly not perfect, I will never win Crufts (get real!) and I have nothing to offer but my time, attention and care. These, however, I try to give freely.

I am who I am – and luckily the people that really matter love me for it.

This is what makes dogs so unique and why we have such a special relationship with you humans. My Think Dog Rules build on these innate doggy qualities and contain everything you need to know to get the most out of life and people, just like me.

TEACHING OLD DOGS!

> Contrary to popular human belief, you can teach an old dog new tricks – and the good news is that the same applies to humans.

The idea that old dogs can't learn new things is simply nonsense. The only way we survived and thrived as hunter/scavengers for thousands of years was through being highly adaptable. That's how we recognised the possibilities offered by humans and took you under our wing all those years ago.

What worked then is still important now and, even though we learn fastest as puppies, we remain flexible in the way we behave throughout our lives. I know it's hard to believe but I've only just started to write books, for instance.

The same is true for humans – you should see Henry and Grace's grandparents use their new computer; mid-seventies (years not months!) and putting some of George's business colleagues to shame.

Whatever you do though, don't be tempted to run before you can manage walkies (we don't want you spraining anything). Remember too that starting something is easy, but keeping it up for the rest of your life – now that is a challenge worthy of a dog! We are all talented but not all of us are disciplined.

There is good news though. With the right insight and some good hard work even the most unruly humans can be tamed.

One final piece of advice: leave this book somewhere that you will see it often – in the loo or by the side of the bed – and then read it at every opportunity. Small bites can sometimes be the best way to tackle a big bone.

Also, why not write to me and let me know what you think or how you are getting on with the rules – visit my website www.thinkdog.net

Well, good luck, my non-furry friends, read the rules and, as we dogs say,
Get dog on it!
Love,
'Dog' (Ludwig)
www.thinkdog.net

THE THINK DOG RULES

The Think Dog Rules come in four chunks – four meaty chunks, if you like.

CHUNK 1

- Don't judge a dog by its collar
- Put your best paw forward
- Be loyal
- Trust is essential
- Make it worth their while
- Show you care

CHUNK 2

- Develop a winning attitude
- Make time
- Keep it simple
- Do as you say
- Stay alert and act decisively
- The buck stops with you

CHUNK 3

- Wag that tail and be happy
- You are the company you keep
- Love something, do something
- Listen and speak their language
- Manage expectations
- Life's not fair

CHUNK 4

- It takes courage
- Lead the pack by example
- Give a dog a good name
- Handle criticism carefully
- Be your own dog
- Every saved relationship enhances YOU

THE RULES

Chunk 1
STARTERS

1.1) DON'T JUDGE A DOG BY ITS COLLAR

> Don't let appearances blind you to interesting possibilities.

First impressions can be very misleading, with some of the most surprising and lasting friendships coming from the most unlikely sources.

To a dog, the most natural thing in the world is to greet another dog with a few enquiring sniffs, regardless of whether they are a Dalmatian like Lucy or a Labrador like Oscar.

We don't care if a dog is black or white or even black and white – or as we would say, Dalmatian! Race, creed and breed count for nothing.

When the first Dalmatians appeared trotting alongside the fine carriages of the aristocracy, they must have looked pretty strange to all concerned, human and dog alike. But just look at them now: Lucy is always a star when she turns up at the park flirting with everyone she meets (but I know she still has a soft spot for me).

No species on earth is as varied as dogs: every dog,

from a tiny Chihuahua like Lola to a huge Saint Bernard like Florence, shares the same genetic footprint.

What dogs have realised is that, regardless of how different we look on the outside, we are almost identical on the inside. From leggy Great Danes to long thin Dachshunds and from gorgeous, elegant Afghans to stubby Bulldogs, we are more alike than we are different.

Outside appearances count for very little. Take Romeo for example: a pink Poodle on the outside but a macho, ladies' dog on the inside. He is as tough and brave as any dog you are likely to meet and gets very upset if any of you humans mistake him for a girl.

Dogs invented the 'pack', or 'team' as you call it, because we recognised that you can't do everything by yourself and if you want to achieve really big things then you are going to need help. Great teams need variety to make them work. Put Florence together with a Jack Russell like Polo and they make a great, if somewhat unusual team.

Next time you are looking for a new friend or partner, think about this: when two people are exactly the same, one of them is unnecessary.

> Or as that well-known human Bill Gates allegedly says:
>   'Be nice to nerds – you'll probably end up working for one!'

@COLLEGE

Break out from your usual group and make friends with someone you would never normally spend time with – they might be great fun.

@HOME

Parents, stop nagging the kids about the small stuff – they'll be gone soon enough and then you'll be sorry.

Kids, remember that your parents weren't born boring – it's coping with you that's done it.

Spend time together and try to learn from each other; you won't always be able to.

@WORK

Spend some time with someone at work whom you usually try and avoid. Try working together on something that isn't a life or death issue, go along with them for a while and see what you can learn.

Who knows? You may become the new Tom and Jerry.

LUCY THE DALMATIAN

Lucy's motto is 'if you've got it flaunt it' – which, coupled to the fact that she is a bit of a flirt, makes her a big hit with the boys.

She is kind hearted, affectionate and easy going most of the time but, like many beautiful ladies, can also be extremely stubborn when she feels like it.

Like me, Lucy is sometimes as much human as she is dog, which makes her a great companion to her human pets, who clearly love her to bits.

1.2) PUT YOUR BEST PAW FORWARD

> You only get one chance to make a first impression so don't waste it waiting for someone else to make the first move.
>
> Act like a dog; put yourself on the line and see what happens.

We spend so much time pussy-footing around (yuk) that sometimes we never show people the real, glorious us and that is a real shame.

Someone can only become genuinely interested in you when they know what you care about, so if you want a real bond to form between you, show them.

Some of the boys that hang around Grace have a tendency to play it safe and put being cool before taking a risk. They spend so long wondering:

- ❀ What if she doesn't like me?
- ❀ What if she laughs at me?
- ❀ Why can't she show me she is interested?

That before they get round to making a move Grace has lost interest and moved on.

To a dog the only cool thing to be is yourself. If you're a Pekingese like Bolton then you 'yap' and if you're a boxer like Edward then you 'woof'; if people like you then great, and if they don't, hey, no big deal, there are plenty more lamp posts down the street.

Have you ever visited a dog rescue centre (or as we prefer to call them 'human adoption centres') run by groups like the Dogs Trust? If you want to understand the importance of making a good first impression then visit one.

The dogs bark, run in and out and jump up and down excitedly on one side of the fence whilst a procession of excited humans 'ooh and aah' on the other side. Both parties have a few seconds to make a lasting and endearing impact before one or the other loses interest and moves on to the next potential love of their life.

Some of the poor dogs you find at these centres have had a terrible time before they were res-cued. I wish they'd let me have five minutes with the people responsible; they wouldn't make the same mistake again.

Dogs are highly sensitive and can take a lot of loving before they recover from any ordeal but, with a kind, loving family to share their life with, most make amazing recoveries.

When Kylie's old pets decided to go back to Australia they left her in England, at a dog rescue centre. There was no way that a dog as cute as Kylie was going to have to wait very long for some new pets but she certainly didn't leave things to chance. After a quick grooming session to make sure that she was looking her best, Kylie went out and strutted her stuff. The first family to visit and bang, it was love at first sight.

Take a leaf out of Kylie's book and, regardless of the situation you find yourself in, put your best paw forward, or as Grace's dance teacher says 'teeth and tits girls, teeth and tits!'

The world's most successful and popular people (and dogs) are natural born networkers who run their social circle as though it is their most valuable asset ...
... Because it is!

@COLLEGE

Don't wait for permission to be yourself and stop worrying about a bit of rejection. If you are not being rejected occasionally then you are not trying hard enough. Winners eat rejection for breakfast; it's how they learn what and who is right for them.

@HOME

Now's the perfect time to go the extra mile – and it doesn't matter whose turn it is, or who owes you what. Just do everyone in the family a favour, without expecting something in return.

Life is way too short to keep a score sheet – and wouldn't you rather be a player than keeping the score or being referee anyway?

@WORK

You know what they say about interviews? The outcome is often decided within the first twenty seconds. Well the same applies to everything at work; People are quick to judge and slow to change.

Don't wait until you need something from someone before giving them the time of day; do them a favour the first chance you get.

KYLIE THE MINIATURE SCHNAUZER

Kylie is a wonderfully spirited and resourceful slip of a dog that would do anything for anyone. She has enough energy to wear even me out and has an amazing 'barking' voice that she uses to sing along to the radio.

Go Kylie go!

1.3) BE LOYAL

> Loyalty runs through dogs like words through a stick of rock. Without loyalty a dog wouldn't be a dog!

To a dog loyalty is probably the most important thing in life next to bones. Some of my doggy mates will go to extraordinary lengths to look after those they love, which is why we cannot understand or tolerate animal cruelty.

Not that loyalty is always easy; it often requires personal sacrifice and putting others before yourself, but that's what being a dog means. Dogs don't take a loyalty holiday when they are busy; they understand that being a friend means being loyal all the time.

The lengths that some of my friends have gone to in order to save their human pets is extraordinary even by my standards. Risking their lives to pull their pets out of burning houses, and diving into rivers to stop them drowning are common stories amongst my canine chums.

I'll never forget the night that Nora attacked two burglars that turned up at her pets' house. She may be small but she wasn't going to let anyone get away with threatening her pets, however big they were. Luckily she made so much noise that Genghis and I heard the row and went to help. I have never seen two humans run so fast, (straight into the police, which was lucky for them because I don't think Nora was in the mood for taking prisoners).

Loyalty is not only about dogs either, I've watched Henry stand up for his friends from time to time and been truly proud. When it comes to his friends, that boy knows no fear.

> Do you aspire to be the best player in the team – or the best team player?

@COLLEGE

Stand up for anyone being bullied and remember that it's harder for someone to bully a whole team. Why not work out who could use some loyalty right now and give them a boost?

@HOME

The opportunities to be loyal at home are endless. Look out for your little brother or sister; don't ignore them, even when they have the potential to be embarrassing.

@WORK

In a time where the emphasis is on instant profit and instant gratification, loyalty can seem harder to achieve in a work context.

But don't let that put you off.

Work out what you can do to demonstrate loyalty at work, and then do it.

NORA THE YORKSHIRE TERRIER

Nora is the perfect friend; she is tough, joyful, lively, inordinately affectionate and bright as a button. She can also be very bossy and quite stubborn, but that is what makes her the wonderful dog that she is.

Nora regularly goes out with her pets and can often be seen with her head sticking proudly out of their shopping bag as she surveys what to her is all part of her estate.

1.4) TRUST IS ESSENTIAL

> Without truth there can be no trust and without trust there can be no peace.

The trust between humans and dogs is based on over 15,000 years of mutual admiration and trust building. Our relationship has seen empires come and go, and civilisations develop and decline, but throughout this entire period the love, friendship and affection exhibited between man and dog has grown and grown.

It is no accident that dogs are now so often referred to as 'man's best friend'. You have proved yourselves over the years by demonstrating amazing intelligence, an ability to kick balls, and a willingness to welcome us into your shelters and share your food with us. For our part we have demonstrated our affection for you in our courage, playfulness, loyalty and resourcefulness.

Nothing in the world is more devoted and trusting than a loving dog and it is a terrible thing if that trust is ever broken.

My friend Winston absolutely adored his old pets and the look in his eyes when they ran off and left him on the streets was awful to see.

Luckily those kind people at the Dogs Trust looked after him until his new pets invited him to share their home.

The great news is that Winston is learning to trust again, but no one, dog or human, deserves to be betrayed like that.

Trust is more easily lost than gained so make sure that people fully understand the reasons for your actions. If a dog is punished for something that it doesn't fully understand it will start to regard all people as unpredictable and unduly aggressive. This may encourage the dog to start snapping at its pets or other humans in self-defence and none of us want that.

Could anything you are doing be having a similar effect on anyone you know?

Trust is fragile; build it carefully, cherish it, and then guard it with your life.

@COLLEGE

College is the sort of place where you either get into a trusting habit or a lying one. Why do you think we dogs have such a bad reputation as homework eaters? Do you actually know a real life dog that has eaten someone's homework? I don't.

Make being trustworthy a lifelong habit; the more you try it the more you'll like it.

Trust me – I'm a dog!

@HOME

Relationships at home are the most important; this is where everyone has the right to trust those around them and if that trust is ever betrayed then everyone loses out.

If you don't want to live in a mad house or a dog house then stick to the truth at home.

@WORK

Trust at work is earned when people consistently tell the truth, yet lying at work is considered par for the course in some organisations, and in some jobs you are even asked or instructed to lie.

My advice is: don't ask others to lie on your behalf and if someone is asking you to lie for them, remember that they will lie to you just as readily.

Life is short; why waste it on people that don't respect you? You'd be better off walking the dog!

WINSTON THE BULLDOG

Despite his somewhat severe appearance Winston is one of the most delightful and kind dogs that I have ever had the privilege of calling a friend.

Nothing makes him happier than rolling around with as many small children as possible climbing all over him or sitting them on a dustbin lid as he pulls it along with his teeth. Hours of fun!

1.5) MAKE IT WORTH THEIR WHILE

> If you want to win someone's heart, make sure that they have a full stomach first!

Dogs and humans aren't much different in this respect. Dogs evolved as opportunistic animals ready to take advantage of any opportunity at the slightest notice, so if you want your dog to be loyal, steadfast and reliable it helps if you make it worth their while.

It is a fundamental law of behaviour applicable to all animals – dogs, humans and even grizzly bears – that when actions are rewarded they will happen more often.

So what are the best ways to make something worthwhile?

Why not try a mixture of the following:

* **A present or reward** – Almost everyone appreciates recognition in the form of a gift. The more thought that has gone into it and the more appropriate or personal the gift the greater the motivational effect it will have.
* **Praise and attention** – Anyone in your pack will enjoy and value any praise that you give them but make sure that you are praising something worth praising, or you may end up scoring an own goal.

* **The opportunity to try a new experience** – Variety is indeed the spice of life and whether it is at college, at home or at work giving someone the opportunity to try something new is a great way to motivate them.

* **Saying thank you** – Belle is not big on showing her emotions but she can be very soppy on occasion.

When her pet lets her travel in the front seat, instead of in the back with the luggage, Belle will sit and stare at him with her big sad eyes for a while before leaning over and giving him a great big lick from his chin to his ear, after that she will turn round and sit with her head out of the window for the rest of the journey.

With this simple gesture she makes her pet feel like a million dollars and can then twist him around her little claw for weeks afterwards!

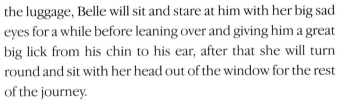

When you make someone do something they will do it reluctantly and not very well.

If you make them want to do it then they will put their heart into it.

@COLLEGE

The key to success with lecturers and teachers is to get them to believe that you are actually listening to their every word. If you can make them feel that they are the 'pack leader' then you can get away with almost anything. Who knows, maybe even the 'Sorry but my dog ate my homework' excuse might work!

@HOME

The key to a happy home is to create a harmonious environment, and then if you ever need to reprimand anyone it will stick out in sharp contrast to the usually happy times.

@WORK

What could be simpler? Make it worth their while and customers and employees will stay with you; take them for granted, exploit or ignore them and off they'll run.

BELLE THE BASSET HOUND

Belle is a gentle dog that just loves to walk and walk. She is surprisingly agile too and really enjoys wandering off on her own, which causes her pets no end of worry and also costs them a fortune in new fencing!

Fiercely proud of her French lineage, she has a sweet voice and I'm sure that I can detect a slight French accent when she barks.

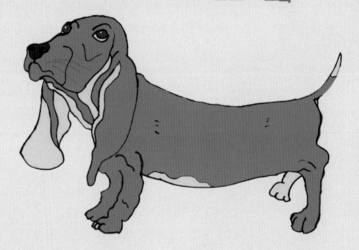

1.6) SHOW YOU CARE

> We all need to feel important and cared for, humans and dogs alike.

Everyone needs to feel loved and appreciated, however high their self-esteem, and we dogs have almost endless ways of showing just how much we care.

Edward the Boxer takes great delight in cocking his leg on his pet's car when she is cleaning it as a show of solidarity. Polo the Jack Russell joins in with the gardening, digging holes in his pets' flower beds as his contribution to the gardening process.

Wally, on the other hand, makes his guests welcome when they arrive at his pets' house by vigorously mounting their leg as a sign of good will. (You should have seen poor Grace blush!)

Now I realise that mounting legs might suit Wally but it isn't the right approach for everyone. Showing appreciation is important though and there are millions of ways to show it.

Being quick to say sorry is one good way – and if you tell me that you never have anything to say sorry for then you are clearly not playing hard enough.

As a highly spirited dog, letting people know I'm sorry from time to time is essential or I'd soon have fewer friends than you could count on one paw.

> Edward plays his part, Polo does his bit and Wally definitely shows he cares, so what are you going to do?

@COLLEGE

I watched two of Henry's friends go through a classic routine the other day. They had had a small tiff in the garden and then both blamed each other. Neither would say sorry and a great day was in danger of descending into a turgid afternoon. If I hadn't had the foresight to nip them both on the backside they would still be moping about it now.

Don't fall into the same trap; big-hearted people show they care, small-minded people bear grudges.

@HOME

Showing you care at home is critical. There is **nothing** worse than seeing families torn apart because of something utterly unimportant that has been allowed to grow and grow to the point that brother stops talking to brother and children lose contact with their parents.

Let's get this straight: very little in life is so important that it is worth breaking a family up for. If there is even a whiff of a problem in your family, do something about it **regardless** of where you think the fault lies.

@WORK

Unresolved disagreements have a nasty habit of causing creeping paralysis in organisations. It starts off with people being less cooperative than they might be but ends in damaging stand-offs.

Result – wasted time, lost money, lost customers and ultimately lost talent.

WALLY THE DACHSHUND

Wally is one of the most devoted dogs I know and for a little chap he has a huge character. I presume they're called Dachshunds because they spend most of their life dashing around; that is certainly what Wally spends most of his time doing.

He's an excitable young fellow with no conception of the words 'no', 'can't' or 'won't fit'. An unforgettable memory is dragging Wally out of a drain pipe in which he had become firmly stuck – a classic Lassie moment.

STRIPPED TO THE BONE: CHUNK 1

These rules may be basic but what a difference they will make to your life.

- **Don't judge a dog by its collar** – first impressions can be very misleading; don't miss out on interesting possibilities.
- **Put your best paw forward** – you only get one chance to make a first impression so don't wait; take it.
- **Be loyal** – loyalty is the ONLY way to keep and grow friendships; end of story!
- **Trust is essential** – without truth there can be no trust and without trust no friendship.
- **Make it worth their while** – don't MAKE them do it; make them WANT to do it and everyone will feel like a winner.
- **Show you care** – when you show people you care they feel better about themselves and want to help you more.

Chunk 2
IMPROVERS

2.1) DEVELOP A WINNING ATTITUDE

 Attitude makes the dog!

Developing a winning attitude is a good way to protect yourself against bullying or offensive behaviour and there is a lot you can learn from dogs on this.

Whether we are talking about college, home or work it makes little difference- the key to avoiding problems of bullying or undue interference is to command respect and maintain an air of confidence and authority.

Gaining the respect of those around you has nothing to do with aggression, but is earned through the consistent demonstration of certain behaviours and values rather than by a few dramatic gestures.

The pecking order within a group or pack is determined by little things which, at first glance, appear to be trivial and insignificant, but which have a major influence in shaping behaviour.

A bully will always target people that they think they can push around – and why will they think that? Because they will have won a series of small confrontations already and feel in a position of power.

Puppies learn this within days of being born and our sniffing routines reinforce it on a daily basis. Lola is the expert at it and despite her small size she never allows herself to be needlessly pushed around by anyone, not even me!

Lola is very assertive and there has never been any chance that her diminutive size could be mistaken for weakness. Just because she is the smallest dog in the world doesn't make her a pushover.

The other key to developing a winning attitude is to maintain a sunny disposition. You may think I've gone a bit soft here, but if you communicate a bright, sunny attitude the whole world is likely to smile back at you.

Maintaining a cheerful, optimistic personality is one of the most important lessons that anyone can learn.

Choose to be happy or choose to be miserable – it's up to you.

As someone once said:

> The right to choose your own attitude can never be taken away ... only surrendered.

@COLLEGE

Nowhere is maintaining a winning attitude more important than at college, where it will help in a number of ways:

- ❦ It will make you more successful.
- ❦ It will keep you out of the way of bullies.
- ❦ It will make you more attractive to the opposite sex.
- ❦ It will put a zing in your step.

Don't give way on little things that you know to be wrong or people will try and push you around on big things. Stand your ground and keep positive at all times.

@HOME

The same as above really.

Everyone is happier when they know where they stand. If a child gets too much of their own way when they are young, they end up insecure and poor at making tough decisions. Treat the kids the way I treat a new puppy and you won't go far wrong.

@WORK

Also as above; too many people at work are happy to accept ordinary as OK and where does it leave them?

Working in ordinary, unexceptional organisations is boring and depressing, so don't let this happen to you; make your organisation (or the bit you work in) extraordinary, not ordinary.

LOLA THE CHIHUAHUA

Don't mistake Lola for a lap dog, she is bright, affectionate and possessive and is a wonderful watchdog for her pets. Despite being one of the smallest dogs in the world, Lola is amazingly alert, active and tough, and seems to believe that she is enormous compared to other dogs. She will stand up to anyone.

If she was MY size she'd be dangerous!

2.2) MAKE TIME

> Visit, play together or make that call while you can. Remember that too many people leave without saying goodbye.

No one – not dogs, parents or children – come with a guarantee that they will be around forever, so use your time wisely having fun with your pets, family and close friends.

When dogs feel lonely or out of sorts they do things like yawning, scratching or barking. Hagrid chases his tail when he is upset or lonely (and sometimes when he gets overexcited as well).

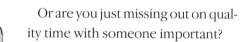

Are you missing any distress signals at the moment?

Or are you just missing out on quality time with someone important?

Why not make today a wonderful day for both yourself and the people you care about? Here is Hagrid's recipe for making today the most wonderful day of your life:

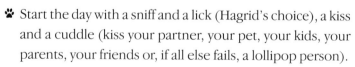

❧ Start the day with a sniff and a lick (Hagrid's choice), a kiss and a cuddle (kiss your partner, your pet, your kids, your parents, your friends or, if all else fails, a lollipop person).

❧ Take a walk just for the hell of it (preferably with your dog).

❧ Laugh or bark out loud.

❧ Hold hands or rub noses (not much fun on your own).

- Touch something you don't normally touch (that's got you thinking).
- Stroke your pets (or talk to them if they are something like a goldfish).
- Eat with someone you care about.
- Show someone that you love them.
- Show someone that you are proud of them.
- If you have a partner, go on a 'date' – don't just go out!
- If you don't have a partner, ask someone out (keep asking until someone says yes).
- If you have kids or a dog, play with them (preferably together).
- Get outside and breathe some fresh air (even in the rain).
- Buy a present for someone.
- Do an unexpected favour.
- Chill out for a while.
- Contact a distant relative.
- Contact a close relative.
- Visit a dog rescue centre.
- Be generous.
- Do something spontaneous.
- Share something naughty but nice.
- Do something for the first time.
- Talk to a neighbour.
- Talk to someone you have never spoken to before.
- Make sure that you look **extra** good.
- Celebrate something.
- Reminisce.
- Make love (if you have someone to do it with).

🐾 Make plans (if you don't).

🐾 End the day with a kiss and a hug (you may well be on really close terms with the lollipop person by now).

Don't let anyone in your life feel lonely or left out. Embrace life the way Hagrid does and make the most of today; you will never get the same chance again.

@COLLEGE

Go out of your way to embrace all the great experiences on offer, but be discerning, because not everything will be quite what it's cracked up to be. Use the Think Dog Rules to decide what is hot and what is not, and make sure that you make every second count.

@HOME

If you don't go and watch the rugby match when your child scores the winning try, or the first dance competition they enter, you may regret it for ever, but you won't regret not doing the ironing or leaving the in-tray half full.

If your parents are in the amateur dramatics go and support them, even if they are mind bogglingly, cringingly embarrassing. That will be you one day.

@WORK

People tend to make time for the big things at work because if they don't, they get fired or go broke. But how about the small things that are more about people than profit?

Write out two lists of things to do today; one list of things that will inspire colleagues and one list of things that will delight your customers. **Repeat this exercise daily.**

HAGRID THE CHINESE CRESTED HAIRLESS

For a little dog Hagrid is food mad and will literally dance around the kitchen, leaping about like a mad dog, at the merest whiff of a biscuit.

I'm forever telling Hagrid to calm down but he doesn't take a blind bit of notice; this dog was born to play!

2.3) KEEP IT SIMPLE

Some dogs might say 'keep everything in life so simple that even a cat can understand it'.
But that would be catist and Puffball and her best friend Alexis would RIGHTLY get upset.

The sentiment is absolutely right though: simplicity makes the dog and can also make the human.

A key difference between dogs and humans is our ability to keep things simple. Dogs like Rufus are strictly route one when it comes to dealing with life's little problems and it saves a great deal of trouble in the long run.

The most important thing in Rufus's life is his pet and he has little time for anything else outside his human family. When he is interested in playing football he will play, when he isn't he asks you nicely in his uniquely Scottish way to leave him alone; no fuss, no frills, no misinterpretation.

But this is not always the case with you humans. I sat back in amazement the other night as Grace came up with a plan to explain why she didn't want to go out with this guy she knew. Three hours, five panicky phone calls, seven texts and nine excuses later, I was still wondering why she didn't just tell him she preferred him as a friend than a boyfriend.

Try not to complicate anything that need not be complicated; simplicity grows on you the more you experience it. After all, complications are the choice of fraudsters, cheats and those without the talent to keep things simple.

Once you have learnt to keep things simple the next lesson is to know when to stop. This is one that even we dogs have to work at.

What is fun to start with can easily become an annoying pain in the neck when it goes on and on. Unfortunately this applies to many of the things that dogs like Rufus and I greatly enjoy, so we have had to adopt the following approach:

Be direct,
Keep it simple,
Lookout for changing levels of interest
And stop before you become annoying or boring!

@COLLEGE

No complicated excuses at college or school please. The best thing to do if you haven't finished your coursework is go and see the teacher before the class. Explain, smile, be good natured and it can work wonders.

But don't overdo it; what you can get away with occasionally will become extremely annoying if you make a habit of it.

@HOME

Repeatedly doing the same things can drive people mad and achieve nothing but frustration. Yes, patience is a virtue, but trying people's patience is not acceptable – even patient dogs have been known to snap when they have their tail pulled for the hundredth time.

@WORK

Dogs constantly communicate with each other; we use all of our senses – sight, sound, smell, etc. – and are therefore very sensitive to anything that changes. Unfortunately this isn't true of humans, particularly in a work situation.

The key to effective relationships is short, sharp, simple, face-to-face meetings with a clear purpose and an understood start, middle and end. If you want to know how to do it, watch a couple of dogs hold a meeting.

We rush up to each other, bark politely, wag our tails for all we are worth, sniff each other to break the ice, first you sniff me, then I sniff you, we bounce around a bit and then bingo, meeting over and on to the next dog.

Try it next time you want something done quickly and effectively.

RUFUS THE SCOTTIE

With Rufus what you see is what you get. Brought up in Glasgow, Rufus is a ten-lampposts-a-night kind of dog and when he wants, or doesn't want something; you know about it.

He is home loving but fiercely independent and what some may feel he lacks in charm (except the ladies who seem to like his direct; 'your basket or mine?' approach), he easily makes up for in openness, loyalty and honesty.

Och aye th-noo!

2.4) DO AS YOU SAY

Are you a class act?
  Because class acts always keep their word, keep their temper and therefore keep their friends!

Nothing in life is more infuriating to a dog than a person who doesn't do what they say they will. It makes Princess want to pull her fur out in frustration if one of her pets promises to go for a walk with her and then forgets or changes their mind because it's raining.

Princess's pets did it to her the other night: six o'clock came and went, and her lead was still hanging there lonelier than a lamppost on a country lane. She could have howled the house down; but she didn't because she is not that kind of dog.

It is not fair and it is not right to create expectations and then fail to meet them. Everybody, both dog and human, deserves reliable friends and when a friend fails the reliability test they fail the friendship test.

If you want to avoid problems in this area the key is not to agree to do things in the first place if you can't deliver them. It is far better to give someone a pleasant surprise than a nasty shock.

One day last week my pets were going out and decided for some reason to leave me at home. They said as they went through the door that they would be back in time for tea and my evening perambulation (walk to you and me).

OK, so I wasn't over the moon about this, but it wasn't too bad. We dogs like some time to chill without you humans fussing around making an awful racket; hoovering, playing music and putting shelves up.

This was the perfect opportunity for me to explore unopened cupboards, and sprawl over the beds and settees that they seem to think they own and somewhat inexplicably prefer me to keep away from.

Two o'clock came and I was just wondering how to while away my afternoon when click went the door and in trooped the whole family. Call me a sentimental, foolish old dog if you like but it was such a great surprise to see them that I went wild with delight, bouncing around and generally giving them the impression that I had missed them.

Had it been the other way round and they'd come home three hours late, then I would have been annoyed. I may even have had to do a quick wee on George's golf shoes as a small sign of protest. (Well, I never said I was perfect!)

So if you say you are going to do something, do it.
    If you can't be 100% sure, err on the side of caution and don't commit to it.

@COLLEGE

When it comes to your study commitments, at least make an effort to do your coursework or homework on time, because whether you do it now or do it later it takes the same amount of time. If you do it now you'll get less hassle and also have less guilt to cope with.

Without being too geeky about it; you only get out of college what you put into it.

@HOME

Parents, if you want a good relationship with your kids then do what you say you will. The amount of resentment that broken promises cause is awful.

If you don't want your kids to let you down when they are older then demonstrate the value of doing what you say now, while you are in a position to influence their value system.

Oh, and kids, for goodness sake, come home when you say you will – you won't believe the number of times I have to hide behind the sofa to avoid Hannah on the war path when Grace comes home late.

@WORK

Most relationship problems at work come down to a loss of trust on the back of failed promises, but keep your word and your most profitable customers, most talented employees and most loyal stakeholders will stick to you like Winston sticks to a bone.

PRINCESS THE AFGHAN HOUND

Princess is the aristocrat amongst us and claims that her ancestors were in the Ark with Noah, which I can believe. As befits her status; She is chic and elegant (not to mention sexy), a bit haughty, impressively dignified and proud of her heritage. I wouldn't be tempted to tease her about Noah and the Ark though because she won't tolerate it.

When you get to know her you will recognise that she is genuinely affectionate, good natured and extremely fit. (Great legs, but don't tell her I said that!)

2.5) STAY ALERT AND ACT DECISIVELY

> In the 21st century, seeing things fast and speed of reaction are vital attributes.

This applies to relationships just as much as anything else, so be on the lookout for how you can help those around you – and when you need to act, do so decisively.

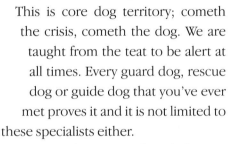

This is core dog territory; cometh the crisis, cometh the dog. We are taught from the teat to be alert at all times. Every guard dog, rescue dog or guide dog that you've ever met proves it and it is not limited to these specialists either.

You ought to see Edward if someone threatens one of his pets. This normally chilled, laid-back and relaxed dog becomes a tower of snarling dog muscle with razor sharp teeth and buckets of slavering drool. (Crikey, I'm scared just imagining it!)

If one of our pets needs help we will be there and we don't wait to be asked, we always have one ear cocked for trouble whatever the time of day.

Never underestimate the importance of body language either; we dogs rely far more on posture to communicate than we do on barking and this is a major area of opportunity for any human too. We can tell whether someone is cross, wants to play, is scared or even what they want us to do just by looking at the way they are standing. This is how we avoid the problems that humans stumble into every day.

When Hannah is worried at work I can tell the moment she walks through the door, but it can take George several broken plates before he even has a clue.

Here's a quick guide to becoming a doggy action hero like Edward:

❀ Read the signs – watch the body language.
❀ Focus – keep your mind and body in one place.
❀ Be tough – don't be a wimp.
❀ Act instinctively (but not impulsively) – you won't always have time to plan.
❀ Be determined – be prepared to make a stand.
❀ Be resourceful – cunning may be needed.

Observation is a wonderful skill, so keep practising and eventually you will be able to predict what is about to happen in any given situation.

@COLLEGE

Watch out for your friends at all times and act fast. Prepare mentally and wait for your time to come. As Louis Pasteur said, 'Chance favours the prepared mind'. (I bet you didn't know I knew that!)

@HOME

There will always be room for improvement on observation in the home because things go unnoticed when you're busy. Keep one eye and one ear open for other family members at all times. If you watch out for changes in their demeanour and attitude, you can be their first line of defence against emotional upsets like bullying, boyfriend and girl-friend trouble and issues at work.

@WORK

You already know you need to be alert to new business opportunities, so extend the same approach to your relationships and watch your fortunes get better and better.

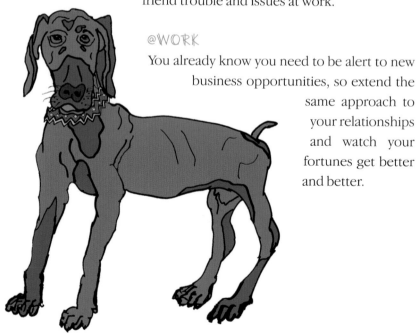

EDWARD THE BOXER

Edward is the consummate athlete and his impressive speed, boundless, almost pup-like enthusiasm and occasionally impetuous nature mean that he can be a bit of a handful to manage, even for me. He is not averse to the occasional scrap with one of his fellow dogs either; it's just his way of letting off steam.

When it comes to humans, however, it's another story; his pets' children can jump on his back and grab on to his ears for all he cares.

2.6) THE BUCK STOPS WITH YOU

> WHATEVER anyone else does or doesn't do, you are always responsible for your own actions.

If something is wrong do something about it; if something important is not being done then do it yourself – don't wait for someone else because they may never come.

No blame, no excuses, no replays.

This is the bottom line for dogs, humans and particularly cats. No one can make you do anything you don't want to do nor can they stop you doing something you are determined to do. It is your choice so choose wisely, my friends.

Dogs know this as well as anyone. Think of all the things that Polo loves to do: chasing cats, ripping up slippers, chewing footballs into tiny pieces, playing tag with postmen. But does he do them all the time? No!

Not to say that there aren't a few rogue dogs out there like there are rogue humans and even rogue lions, but at the end of the day all of us have to be responsible for what we do.

When Polo is playing in the park and gets the urge to run off with the kids' football he has to count to three, breathe deeply, think about bones or lady dogs for a while, and usually the temptation passes and peace reigns. If Polo can do it so can you.

If you don't want anyone else to dictate how you behave then you need to be clear about your own values and goals. Only by knowing what is right for you can you make the right decisions.

❧ What do you believe in?
❧ What are your values?
❧ What are your goals?
❧ What are your decision-making criteria?

Once you know what you want to do and what you believe in, stick to it absolutely. We dogs invented persistence (or doggedness), which is why you named it after us.

Allegedly, more than 99% of human ideas go nowhere and 99% of human talent goes undeveloped. Now I know that human talent isn't in quite the same league as canine talent, but what a waste.

> Successful people, like successful dogs, make a habit of the things that failures don't like to do.

@COLLEGE

What you do now will shape your whole life so make the most of your time at college. It's not so much what you learn, because you will keep learning right throughout your life; it's the attitudes you develop that are important.

Make a list of the things you believe in, the things you want to achieve in life and the key ways you want to behave, then read the list every morning when you wake up.

@HOME

No one is better placed to turn your house into a loving, supportive home than you. Whatever your age, you can take responsibility for it. (If you need some extra help, try getting a dog to adopt your family.)

@WORK

Too many people avoid taking personal responsibility at work by saying that it is not in their job description, they are not paid enough or there is someone else who should do it.

What a waste of life and opportunity. Talent has a million homes so now is a great time to break out of your comfort zone – do something a bit daring, challenge yourself and do something you will be proud of.

POLO THE JACK RUSSELL

Wonderful, generous and excitable, Polo is into absolutely everything, has tireless energy and for some reason known only to him, often runs on only three legs.

Polo is great with his pets, teaching them the basics of football and involving them in everything he does.

Personality 10, discipline 0.

STRIPPED TO THE BONE: CHUNK 2

Now you have read Chunk 2 you should not only be thinking like a dog, you should start to behave like a dog. Good times are on the way.

- **Develop a winning attitude** – if you want to get the most out of life then think like a winner.
- **Make time** – time is precious so spend it with those you love, those that need you.
- **Keep it simple** – complications kill relationships so keep everything simple, straight and above board.
- **Do as you say** – integrity is the backbone of life; only make promises if you are willing and able to keep them.
- **Stay alert and act decisively** – keep your eyes open for ways to help and when you spot an opportunity take it.
- **The buck stops with you** – you are responsible for EVERYTHING you do or don't do; no one else.

ADVANCED

3.1) WAG THAT TAIL AND BE HAPPY

> Every time you argue with someone they could end up disliking you and you could end up losing a friend, so remember to pick your arguments carefully.

Close your eyes and think about your favourite dog for a moment. Now I bet the dog you are thinking of has a wagging tail and a happy face!

We dogs are past masters at tail wagging. And you know what? It works. Dogs and humans alike are a soft touch to a wagging tail; Oscar, for example, can charm the pants off whoever he meets without even opening his mouth. I have never met a happier dog than Oscar, a handsome, wondrously smiley face at one end, a fantastic super-waggy tail at the other and a great big heart in the middle – what a superb package!

OK, so you humans are at a bit of a disadvantage not having a tail, but all is not lost: what you lack in a tail you can make up for with body language.

Smile with your whole face, let those lovely eyes of yours sparkle, feel happy on the inside and it will start to radiate out.

Smiling costs nothing; it is a sign of confidence and people like to be around confident, successful people. Smiling increases your face value; it makes you feel good and makes other people feel good.

Shouting, on the other hand, makes people resentful, stops them hearing what you are trying to say and makes them want to shout back at you.

Result – chaos.

Driving around with my pets I get to see a great deal of road rage, which if I'm honest (and being a dog I am) probably has quite a lot to do with George's driving.

But it's not just George. Many humans seem to go mad when they get behind the wheel of a car, driving like lunatics and snarling at every passing car (not to mention the gesticulating). This is very un-dog-like behaviour; when was the last time you saw a dog driving badly?

It is important to recognise when someone is getting angry. Angry humans are just like dogs: they become still and stiff just before they snap. If you think someone is getting angry, back off a bit and let them have some space or time on their own. The adrenalin produced by anger takes time to wear off, so let people calm down before trying to sort things out.

If you feel yourself getting angry, try and look at things from the other person's point of view (and that means getting down on your hands and knees if you are arguing with a dog), keep your sense of humour and be prepared to be wrong occasionally.

Avoid forcing anyone into a corner or they will have no choice but to come out fighting; and have the good grace to stop before your opponent becomes your life-long enemy.

@COLLEGE

Smile at teachers and lecturers, smile at the other students, remain calm and serene at all times and create your own oasis of goodwill.

Write down in your 'Friends Log' every time you achieve a breakthrough result through smiling and looking happy.

@HOME

Think about your grumpiest relative and try a charm offensive on them. Be happy regardless of what they throw at you (hopefully metaphorically not physically). If all else fails, buy them a copy of *Think Dog* and try again later.

Relationships with neighbours are another potential problem area so be careful what you argue about – you don't want your life descending into a running battle.

@WORK

Be reasonable and understanding with people today; you never know whose support you might need tomorrow.

Try smiling at everyone you meet from when you leave your door to when you get home. Find the most miserable person at work and be relentlessly cheerful. Mount your own crusade to turn them into a happy, smiley person.

If you feel really strongly about something find better ways of handling it than direct confrontation.

OSCAR THE LABRADOR

Of all my friends, Oscar is probably the most reliable and when he has just been for a swim in the river, which he does often because he loves it, he can always be relied upon to shake his coat vigorously right next to his pets.

He is incredibly straightforward, honest and kind. Two of his family became guide dogs, which doesn't surprise me because, like Oscar, they are patient and understanding and rarely get into trouble.

A great friend in times of trouble, good on you Oscar!

3.2) YOU ARE THE COMPANY YOU KEEP

Hang out with people who share your beliefs, who believe in **you** and who believe in themselves.

Or alternatively, as Darcy found out the other day when he went on a farm holiday with his pets: if you mix with dogs who have fleas, you will catch fleas.

When someone decides that they would like to be adopted by a new puppy they usually think long and hard about what type of puppy would suit them best. They realise that, however cute a puppy looks now, if it is going to grow up to be over a metre tall and to need a ten mile walk every day, and they live in a small flat, then there are going to be problems.

You need to apply the same logic in selecting your friends because the company you keep will directly affect your whole life.

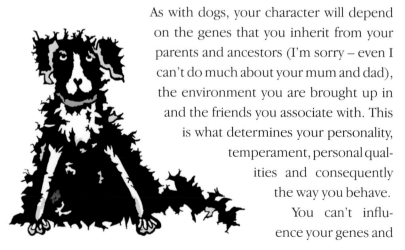

As with dogs, your character will depend on the genes that you inherit from your parents and ancestors (I'm sorry – even I can't do much about your mum and dad), the environment you are brought up in and the friends you associate with. This is what determines your personality, temperament, personal qualities and consequently the way you behave.

You can't influence your genes and

you may not be able to do much about your environment, but you can choose your friends, which is why they are so important.

Consider this:

* **friends influence behaviour,**
* **behaviour turns into habits,**
* **habits define character,**
* **character shapes destiny.**

Hence you are the company you keep.

Things that you do on a regular basis rapidly become habits and, before you know it, they dominate the way you respond to every new situation. The problem with habits is that they are hard to change and sometimes you have to really work at changing them. One thing you can do, though, is change your friends – if they are influencing you in the wrong way then maybe it is time to move on.

If you want to keep growing as a person you must be willing to let go of friendships that are holding you back or leading you astray. You must also be prepared to let other people go when they feel the need to move on.

If you part on good terms who knows what may happen if your paths cross again? (I'd certainly like to be reintroduced to that flirty young Greyhound I met in the park last month!)

> Don't drown your sorrows over friendships that have run their course; accept the gift of goodbye and move on.

@COLLEGE

Don't be afraid to say no or step back from a friendship if it starts to compromise what you believe in.

It is very easy to fall for a cute face but do ask yourself if you would want them as the mother or father of your puppies.

@HOME

How far should you go in expressing your views about your kids' friends? Consider these points before deciding what to do:

❤ You don't want to alienate yourself from your children.
❤ You cannot make their decisions for them all their life.
❤ What is right for you isn't always right for them.

The most important things you can give your children are your love, your time, self belief and a good values system, so don't undermine these things by the way you deal with one issue.

If you listen to and respect your children's opinions when they are younger, they will be much more likely to listen to you when they are older.

@WORK

You don't have to like everyone you work with but make it a rule only ever to work closely with people you respect.

DARCY THE BORDER COLLIE (THE FLEAS HAVE GONE NOW, BY THE WAY!)

Darcy is the wild child of our bunch and is totally 'out there'. More at home in the sea, on the beach or out in the country, Darcy is certainly not scared of hard work but also believes that life is for living.

If he could choose his pet's car he would definitely go for a VW Camper Van and often talks about going to live in a commune.

3.3) LOVE SOMETHING, DO SOMETHING

> If you want to be great at something you have to love it with all your heart.

Do you know why Genghis is such a great dog?

Because he loves every moment of his life, he loves his pets, his friends, he loves lady dogs, he loves the park, he loves dog biscuits – he is even fond of Puffball and Alexis.

Genghis embraces doggyness in every waking moment of his life – he is a dog from start to finish. He eats dog, sleeps dog, lives dog! Being a Great Dane is the only thing in the whole world that Genghis ever wanted to be.

Can you say the same about your life? Are you doing something that you are really proud of, something that you really love and something that you are happy to put all of your energy and more into? Is it something that you will be remembered for in time to come?

What is your dream, what are you passionate about? Is it the focus of your life or have you tucked it away somewhere in the corner of your mind while you get on with day-to-day monotony?

What is your favourite song: 'raindrops keep falling on my head' or 'I did it my way'?

There will always be someone out there who will be negative about your ideas and insult what you are trying to do, but don't let that get you down. Small minded people never get on and do great things.

On the other paw, it is wise at least to listen to what other people have to say; you don't have to change what you are doing but you might just learn something – just because you can do something doesn't mean that it is the right thing for you to do.

Dogs like Genghis can stand on two legs but they don't do it all the time because it is not what they are best at.

@COLLEGE

Resist any pressure to become something you are not. They kept telling Grace that she would make a good lawyer but she thought 'That's not me, I want to paint and create things', which is why she is now at art school not law school. (A narrow escape I think!)

Get to know your own strengths and weaknesses; winners are brutally honest about themselves and know that life is too short to make all their own mistakes, so learn as much as you can from other people.

@HOME

There has to be room at home for EVERYONE to do their own thing and no one should have to sacrifice their dreams just to make life easier for everyone else.

If you are yet to do something that you have always wanted to do, then now is the time to get on with it. It doesn't matter whether it is going back to college, skydiving, nude rambling or ballroom dancing; no more excuses, start it today.

@WORK

Some people love their jobs, live life to the full, exude energy and send out positive vibes to their family and friends.

Other people stick in jobs they loathe, sleepwalk through life from morning to night, fail to develop their true potential and therefore have nothing extra to offer those they love and care about.

And what is the difference between them?

Bravery.

So what are you: a dog or a mouse?

GENGHIS THE GREAT DANE

We all know someone like Genghis; a gentle giant, strong as an ox but with an amazingly kind and gentle heart.

Don't make the mistake of confusing kindness with softness, however, because Genghis has a strong sense of fair play and if he sees anyone being teased or bullied he will quickly step in and 'sort it'.

As much at home with his pets as he is with his dog friends, I feel honoured to be able to count Genghis as one of my pack.

3.4) LISTEN AND SPEAK THEIR LANGUAGE

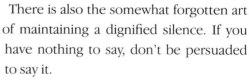

I speak English but do you speak Dog?

People sometimes say 'sticks and stones can break my bones, but words can never hurt me'. If only this were true; the reality is that words are powerful weapons that can do awful damage.

Think carefully about everything you say, because words have a nasty habit of either hanging around long after you wish they had been forgotten, or being forgotten way before they have been properly understood.

As important as what you say is the way you say it. Tone of voice can convey all sorts of things, like what mood you are in, how urgent something is and whether you are pleased or angry. As a dog I learn as much about what people are saying to me from the tone of their voice as I do from listening to the actual words,

There is also the somewhat forgotten art of maintaining a dignified silence. If you have nothing to say, don't be persuaded to say it.

When it comes to listening, remember that although human hearing isn't bad it certainly isn't dog-like. We can hear things at least five times better than you can and we can listen to frequencies beyond the range of your ears.

We all need to understand the limitations of other people and communicate in a way they understand. If I try and communicate with you ultrasonically, for example, then neither of us is going to make much progress.

Observing my humans has also taught me that you can talk about three times as fast as you can listen.

To complicate things further, males like my doggy friend Rufus and my human pet George are what you might call 'solvers', but females like Gerri, Hannah and Grace are sharers.

When Hannah talks to George about the problems she is facing at work he is off solving them in his head after about ten seconds, when all Hannah wants is for him to sit and listen. This is why George and I spend so much time in the dog house together.

Listening is a great skill that many dogs have mastered to perfection. People are mesmerised by good listeners, which is why good doggy listeners like Gerri are so popular and why good human listeners are rarely short of a friend or partner.

Gerri can tune into her pets' emotional wavelength with ease and reads people's moods like a mind reader. She knows precisely when a boisterous greeting is in order, when to sit and listen, and when to stare encouragingly, nuzzling up at appropriate moments.

So how do you become a good listener?

- ❖ Listen with your eyes.
- ❖ Listen for thoughts and feelings.
- ❖ Listen for the silences.
- ❖ Listen with an open mind.

@COLLEGE

Take time out to listen and you will grow in popularity over-night. Don't interrupt people – let them finish before you start talking. Think about what other people have said before answering and show that you respect their opinions and their right to express them.

Basic but powerful stuff.

@HOME

Many problems at home start because of what is not being said. When people are sad, lonely or worried they normally hope you will notice before they have to tell you them-selves.

Keep your eyes and ears open and give people a decent chance to express their true feelings and concerns.

@WORK

When you get back to work keep a record of how often you communicate for a week. The following week spend twice as long communicating and the week after that increase it by the same amount again. Don't forget that communication is a two-way process and involves more listening than talking.

GERRI THE BICHON FRISE

When I can't find Gerri I usually go down to the beauty parlour and there she is. I wouldn't say she's vain but she does believe in looking her best (not that I'm complaining).

Gerri is my confidant and when she looks at me with those big expressive eyes I can tell her anything.

3.5) MANAGE EXPECTATIONS

> If you want valuable, lasting relationships, set clear and reasonable expectations from the start.

Communicate your ideas, listen to people's reactions and adjust your thinking as necessary. Be prepared to change your expectations if circumstances change.

When Bolton rushes up to another dog and does all that sniffing and rushing around inspecting the other dog's bits this is what he's doing. Each dog needs to know where they stand in the doggy pecking order so that we can all get on with having a fun, peaceful time.

Any self-respecting dog like Bolton also understands the importance of teaching young puppies respect. He never lets an overexcited pup use its teeth and claws on him because it sends out the wrong signals and confuses the puppy.

We take the same approach with our pet humans. Each of my pets knows exactly what is expected of them. George knows that I expect him to feed me, Hannah knows that I expect her to come out for a walk with me every day (it's good for her anyway). Grace knows to give me some cuddles every evening and Henry knows that it is his job to play with me in the garden and provide balls for me to chew into tiny pieces.

There you are – one nice happy family with clear, understood expectations.

If you want sound relationships, follow these guidelines:

❀ Set boundaries – let people know right from the start what you expect and don't expect.
❀ Value other peoples opinions – always wise.
❀ Feel for people – use your heart as well as your head.
❀ Pull your weight – even when you are tired.
❀ Be open and direct – no silly games or prevarication, please.
❀ Build up a clear understanding of other people's motivations – dogs and humans are motivated by very different things; lampposts probably mean a great deal more to me than they do to you, for example.
❀ Show appreciation often – dogs love it, kids love it; boyfriends, girlfriends, wives and husbands demand it.
❀ Be reasonable – a shy, submissive dog is unlikely ever to turn into a super-confident extrovert like me and neither is a really shy human ever likely to become a wild party person.

Be realistic about your own and other people's limitations.

@COLLEGE

Be clear about where you stand on things; for example, you don't want any unwanted romantic complications arising with people you only see as friends; it will only result in someone getting hurt and that will damage your reputation.

If, on the other paw, you are up for a little more than a chat, you need to let them know that as well, or you might end up home alone on prom night and that won't do.

@HOME

Be a parent first and a friend second. Children have lots of friends but only one mum and dad.

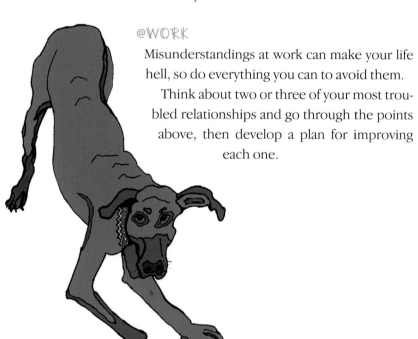

@WORK

Misunderstandings at work can make your life hell, so do everything you can to avoid them.

Think about two or three of your most troubled relationships and go through the points above, then develop a plan for improving each one.

BOLTON THE PEKINGESE

Bolton is a dog full of apparent contradictions, as happy wading through a muddy field as he is at home being pampered by his pets. He can be a bit irritable at times though and is best given a wide berth when he's feeling grumpy.

  Not easily put off, one of the funniest things I have ever seen was Bolton trying to get amorous with Princess, the Afghan! Now they would have been interesting puppies ...

3.6) LIFE'S NOT FAIR

> They call it a 'dog eat dog world', which I can't help thinking is the pot calling the kettle black!

We dogs never eat each other. In fact we have a very reliable and gentle method of sorting out a pecking order in our pack. You humans, though, can be ruthless when it comes to fighting your way to the top and doing whatever needs to be done. Some of the things that go on in George's office are plain wrong. Much worse than dogs.

We dogs have our weaknesses (if you want more on this topic talk to Puffball – she has a degree in it!) but expecting life to be totally fair isn't one of them.

We expect people to be unreasonable, illogical and self centred but love them anyway. This is fundamental to the dog psyche, central to the Think Dog Rules and a key thing for you to think about.

We are used to living in an unfair world. For a start, most of the interesting things in life go on above our head. You should spend a day on your knees and then you would know what it feels like. Maybe then you would be a bit more understanding when we dogs get frustrated.

Some people, though, are able to take it on the chin. Dogs like Romeo and some humans like Henry have mastered the knack of blowing life's problems away; whatever life, or other people, throw at them they simply rise above it.

Romeo isn't put off when someone lets him down, regardless of why it is. It doesn't matter to him whether someone has simply made a mistake or acted out of plain ignorance, anger, greed or stupidity. He never avoids a problem but deals with it head on, forgives those that ask for it and then moves on to the next opportunity.

He is much happier for it too. Being pink he has every reason to grumble about how unfair life is but he doesn't, he embraces the challenge and looks at the upside. (He says that at least his stomach doesn't brush the ground like Wally the Dachshund!)

So, be like Romeo; take it on the chin, live for today and make your excitement about the good stuff stronger than your moaning about the bad.
Life is short – eat more biscuits!

@COLLEGE

Don't focus on what you think life owes you; concentrate on what you can do for yourself, and then get on with achieving it.

Don't hesitate to seek help when you need it, but don't be a moaner or a whinger.

@HOME

The concepts of fairness and home go together about as well as cat and dog but luckily that doesn't matter. Do your best to help out and it will encourage everyone else to do the same.

If someone isn't pulling their weight, get your pack together and nicely point out the error of their ways.

@WORK

Work isn't about fairness, it is about effectiveness; so create a win–win situation and everyone will benefit: customers and colleagues alike.

ROMEO THE POODLE

Despite his unusual colour, Romeo is very much a dog's dog. He is amazingly vivacious, playful and loyal and has a wicked sense of humour.

But a dog's life isn't easy when you're pink and Romeo's favourite phrase is 'poo happens!' He has learned the importance of being tough and resilient because he has had to be and I think he's a better dog for it.

Romeo is now a great friend of mine and massively popular with the rest of the pack.

STRIPPED TO THE BONE: CHUNK 3

Mastery of Chunk 3 will bring you friends, happiness and contentment in abundance. Now you have completed the chunk, expect to buy a bigger diary – you are entering a social whirl.

❧ **Wag that tail and be happy** – don't be a mad dog; cheerful, reasonable people are more popular and more successful.

❧ **You are the company you keep** – people you spend time with will either enhance or damage you so pick your friends wisely.

❧ **Love something, do something** – if you want the most out of life spend it doing something you love.

❧ **Listen and speak their language** – words are amazingly powerful so listen carefully and speak clearly.

❧ **Manage expectations** – let people know what to expect and you will avoid upsets and disappointments later on.

❧ **Life's not fair** – it's a dog eat dog world out there so be prepared to face the worst and go for it.

DOG-LIKE

4.1) IT TAKES COURAGE

> 'Courage is what it takes to stand up and speak ...
> ... courage is also what it takes to sit down and
> listen.'
>
> Winston Churchill

The two words 'courage' and 'dog' are almost interchangeable. Courage is just what we do.

It took real courage for Nora my Yorkshire Terrier chum to stand up to an Alsatian that was worrying her pets on the beach and there are endless stories from the past where brave dogs have stood up to wolves in order to protect their pets.

But courage is about more than just bravery: it takes courage to stand up for your beliefs, to tell a friend what they need to hear and to say, 'Yes I was wrong', when required.

Puffball our cat is courageous. She lives in a world dominated by me and my doggy chums on one hand and by our human pets on the other but she still remains totally true to her cat nature.

She is independent and sassy and stands up for her cat rights when she needs to. She calls a spade a shovel and will tell anyone – human, Doberman or St Bernard alike – exactly what she thinks. If another cat tries to step on her paws you ought to see the fur fly. I have learnt a lot about courage from Puffball and her best friend Alexis.

> Stand up for your friends when they need you and stand up to them if you think they are taking the wrong path or leading you astray.

@COLLEGE

As well as being one of the most exciting times of your life, college is also when you will be open to maximum temptation and risk. Learn to be courageous now, stick up for yourself, do what you know to be the right thing and it will stay with you forever.

@HOME

Love and courage are an extremely powerful combination, so next time you face a challenge at home rise up and meet it. If you work together to face something as a pack, like we do, then you can do pretty much anything.

@WORK

There are endless opportunities to show courage at work but a yearning for security can lead them to pass unnoticed. When you have the courage of your own convictions and you follow your inner beliefs, it enhances you, your job and all those around you.

PUFFBALL THE FLUFFY FARM CAT AND ALEXIS THE ORIENTAL SHORTHAIR

I am not an expert on cats but I think Puffball's farm cat mother mixed in some pedigree company. (Puff seems to think so anyway – as far as she is concerned she is definitely descended from cat royalty!) She expects nothing but the best, is as tough as they come and takes no back chat from anyone, despite the fact that she looks like a ball of fur on legs.

Inquisitive, sociable and cheeky, Alexis is a different kettle of fish altogether; sleek, and slender, she is a mischievous little miss and as slippery as St Bernard slobber.

Puff and Alexis are very much part of our 'crew' and prove that you can form wonderful and surprising friendships in the least likely places.

4.2) LEAD THE PACK BY EXAMPLE

> People support the underdog but follow the top dog.

We dogs understand packs and leadership from the moment we are born. We know that leadership is expressed in every movement we make, in every glance, in every twitch of a muscle, and that you have to demonstrate leadership rather than demand obedience.

Both people and dogs are generally happier when they have a strong leader to protect and guide them, as long as that leader is considerate and understanding rather than overbearing.

Everyone has the potential to become a leader and as long as they remember that it is more about sacrifice than privilege then there is no reason why they won't do an excellent job. Why do you think that we dogs let you humans eat the best meat and sleep in the softest beds?

You don't need to be a leader all the time though – sometimes it is enough just to be a useful member of the pack. Jemima only discovered that she was a great leader when she had puppies. Until then she had been happy to go with the flow most of the time, but the arrival of six boisterous balls of uncontrolled energy changed all that. And what a

great leader she makes too – I have never seen a better organised litter of pups; she would make a few Sergeant Majors proud.

As a leader, the way you are feeling will transmit to all those around you. Take Jemima, for example: if she is anxious then her pups become anxious, but when she's happy they are all happy, lively and full of fun.

It just goes to show that when you get on and demonstrate leadership qualities, those around you will naturally follow.

It doesn't matter what Jemima says to her pups, they always copy what she does.

@COLLEGE

College is a perfect leadership training ground. It's great to try official positions like running a committee, leading the students' union, etc., but you can also learn a lot by simply leading your friends or captaining a sports team.

@HOME

Give me the puppy and I'll give you the dog. Parents have the best opportunity in the whole world to be leaders, but leadership in the home isn't restricted just to adults; everyone can be the leader when necessary.

There have been several occasions when Henry has told everyone to take a chill pill because he felt things were getting out of hand.

@WORK

You don't need to be a boss to be a leader – just know your own strengths and weaknesses, be well informed about your customers, colleagues and partners, and consistently try to help people to achieve what needs to be done.

JEMIMA THE BULL TERRIER

Jemima was born to be a mum. She is devoted to her pups and gathers cushions, rugs and anything soft such as jumpers from all around the house to make a nest for them to lie down in. Anyone that thinks Bull Terriers are ugly should see her with her puppies: they are so gorgeous that seeing them together makes even a big, strong dog like me go all soppy.

Although too strong for some pets to deal with, she is the softest dog you have ever met and when she doesn't have her own pups to look after she gathers together her pets' children and looks after them instead.

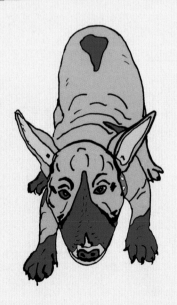

4.3) GIVE A DOG A GOOD NAME

Praise, encouragement and more praise.

You humans are pretty good at encouraging us when you want to be, it's 'good girl' this and 'good girl' that every time Portia performs even a menial task like fetching a stick or putting her paw out to be shaken.

And I get more cuddles from Grace for fetching her slippers than her boyfriend gets for taking her for a nice meal. (By the way, for a dog that can understand 12 human languages, fetching slippers isn't rocket science.)

What amazes me is that you don't apply the same principles to each other. Humans actually need more praise than dogs, because on the whole you are more insecure – but unfortunately you tend to get less than we do.

If George gave Hannah half the attention he gives me then she would be over the moon!

Break with your old habits and start treating those around you the way Portia and I are treated. Start spreading the 'good boys' and 'good girls' around but *please* use some more imaginative language, because even dogs get bored of the well-intentioned, condescending approach.

People love to be appreciated: just a 'thank you' can make all the difference! Some people do a whole lifetime's great work (like the good folk that run the dog rescue centres) and never receive the amount of thanks they deserve.

> The more thanks and encouragement you give to others the more you'll get back.
>   The more pleased you are the more I will want to please you.
>   These are core dog principles.

@COLLEGE

People put other people down to cover up their own insecurities; if you can make someone feel better about themselves they won't feel the need to do it. They might even start to encourage people instead.

Decide who has been having a hard time recently and do your best to talk them up a bit. Who knows – you might start a Mexican wave of encouragement, right around the college.

@HOME

The effect of a few kind words at home can be amazing. Encourage your brothers, sisters, sons and daughters and, as they grow in confidence, they will be more and more able to help you.

Try and remember that parents need encouragement from time to time as well. I know they pretend to have all the answers but they don't, they are only big kids at heart.

@WORK

Everyone at work should both have a mentor and be a mentor to someone else. Encouraging other people helps you grow and learn at the same time.

Just think how much you could learn from getting to know and understand your dog better.

PORTIA THE WEIMARANER

Portia is probably the most learned of us dogs and if there is anything we don't know then Portia is our first port of call. Portia is one of my key lieutenants – we have a special bond because one of my grandparents was a Weimaraner. Could that explain why I am not quite as daft as I look?

Portia comes from a large family and when some of her brothers and sisters come to visit, they make a fine sight wandering around together in their wonderfully coloured coats. (They are my most sophisticated friends!)

4.4) HANDLE CRITICISM CAREFULLY

> Constructive criticism is an integral part of life and an essential part of learning, sharing and growing.

A real friend will tell you what you **need** to hear, not what you **want** to hear, but if any criticism is going to work it needs to be constructive.

Even poor old Sally has to cope with being told she's a naughty girl from time to time (yes, I know it's hard to believe when you look into those big brown eyes).

Sally has a bit of a problem though: whenever she is worried or frightened she can't help barking – sometimes she will bark all day. But if one of her pets loses patience and gets cross with her it only makes matters worse. She only barks when she is upset and can't understand why she is told off for it – all she really needs is a cuddle.

The solution in these situations is to understand why the dog or human is doing whatever they are doing and then spend time with them to solve the problem.

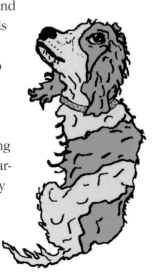

How often have you seen the same thing happening with humans and their children? Parents shouting at children for getting in the way when all they really want is more time with their mum or dad, or to be told they are loved. It makes me cross when this happens, because it is totally unnecessary.

Next time you are thinking of criticising someone, ask yourself a few questions before you start:

- ☙ Are you too tired or emotional to do the job properly?
- ☙ Is it the right time and place?
- ☙ Do you know the person (or indeed the dog) well enough for them to be able to accept criticism or advice from you?
- ☙ Do they trust you enough to listen?
- ☙ Are you qualified or experienced enough to criticise?
- ☙ Are you the BEST person to help?

And always try to:

- ☙ address the problem not the person or dog;
- ☙ avoid unhelpful comparisons;
- ☙ provide positive, creative ways forward.

And remember that:

It takes twelve compliments to balance the effect of one heartfelt criticism (humans and dogs are the same on this).
   So think before you criticise.

@COLLEGE

Be careful about criticising others and think long and hard about the criticism you receive. The better you know yourself the better you can handle criticism coming your way. Don't be too proud to listen, but never be put off from what you know is right for you.

@HOME

Delivering criticism well is a key part of being a parent and must not be shied away from, but destructive criticism will kill your relationship with your children, destroy their confidence and dramatically reduce your long-term influence over their lives.

Effective praise for the right things will have the reverse effect.

Enough said.

@WORK

Think about the fact that it takes twelve compliments to balance one criticism.

What is the ratio where you work?

What can you do to improve the situation?

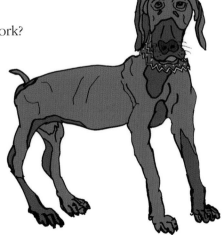

SALLY THE KING CHARLES

Sally is afraid of nothing except being on her own. She is very refined and dignified as befits her royal status, but this doesn't stop her having fun or getting stuck into our games when she feels like it. You should see the look on the face of a new dog to our pack when this innocent looking, ladylike dog starts telling naughty jokes.

No neighbourhood barbeque or party would be complete without Sally to add a bit of sauce to the proceedings.

4.5) BE YOUR OWN DOG

> Why be a fake when 99.9% of the new ideas in the world never get to see the light of day?

What is the point in nicking someone else's ideas and leaving your own originals going begging?

Every dog is a one off, which is why being a bit of a mongrel is far better that being a purebred. It would have been too easy to have been a pure-bred Doberman – and would I have been this handsome? I don't think so.

They may not want me at Crufts but am I bothered?

Do I look bothered?

Not a bit of it! Why be a copycat (sorry, Puff) when you can be a unique, one-off dog?

This is why Bloodhounds like Arthur don't bother trying to be something they are not, but get on with what they do best, which is following tracks. 2500 years of breeding have made him the dog he is today and he isn't interested in pulling sledges or racing around after hares.

If you want to get the most out of life, keep looking till you find something that suits you and that you love to bits – and make sure you know yourself well enough to recognise it when you see it.

You will only be the very best you can be when you are doing the thing that you were born to do best. Discovering what that is and sticking to it may require you to 'howl out of tune' for a while, even when everyone around you is telling you not to give up the day job. A dog will always be a dog even if it is living in a cattery (Heaven forbid), so be careful who you listen to and try not to get distracted by unnecessary and unrealistic comparisons; after all, there is no one else in the world, quite like you.

Learn to encourage yourself, focus on your potential not your limitations and avoid beating yourself up about small stuff.

There is no advantage in being negative about yourself; there are more than enough people out there to do that for you.

@COLLEGE

Write a list of:

* five great things about you
* five things you are brilliant at (there will be at least five)
* five amazing dreams for what your future could look like
* five people that have inspired you or that you admire
* five things (principles, beliefs, values, goals) that you believe in.

Ask a couple of people whom you respect and who know you well to do the same exercise on your behalf. Write the answers down on a large piece of paper and work out what connects everything.

Set about making it your life's work.

@HOME

Repeat the above exercise for each member of your family and think about how you can help them live life to the max.

@WORK

Are you in the right job? Because now is the perfect time to do something about it if you're not.

If you are in the right job then what can you do to use your special skills and abilities to even greater advantage?

Is there any training that would help you to achieve more?

If so, then either organise it yourself or ask for it. Keep on asking until you get it – and if you don't get it then ask yourself again, 'Am I really in the right job?'

ARTHUR THE BLOODHOUND

I don't know what it is about my friends, but they all seem to be great with human kids and Arthur is no exception. My pets got into a terrible tizz a while ago when Henry disappeared and no one could find him anywhere. 'I know', I thought, 'we need Arthur', so off I went to get him.

After a quick sniff of one of Henry's trainers (a braver dog than me), off he went. An hour later we had all followed Arthur across the great big orchards behind the house and there was Henry, with his bears (not real ones) Fuzz and Congo for company, having a picnic in a den he had built out of old pallets. Boy, were we pleased to see him, and Arthur was given a massive chewy thing as a reward.

4.6) EVERY SAVED RELATIONSHIP ENHANCES __YOU__

> EVERY relationship is important – even seemingly meaningless interactions can strengthen or damage your reputation.

OK, I'll hold my paws up (not all four at the same time or I'll fall over) and admit that none of my rules are rocket science.

Actually, I'm happy to go much further than that and say I'm proud of the fact that they are not rocket science. They are so simple that even a five-month-old puppy or a five-year-old child can understand them – and deliberately so. If they can understand them, there is no excuse for you not to.

When you fix a damaged relationship it makes your life better. But every damaged relationship in your life, however tiny and apparently insignificant, damages you. You may never find out exactly what effect a broken or lost relationship has on your life, but opportunities to meet new people and try new things that would otherwise have come your way simply won't happen, and that can be a real shame.

Florence was born understanding this rule, and knew from the moment she opened her eyes and started wandering around that every good relationship she developed would make her a better, happier dog.

Florence is a rescue dog, a fabulous St Bernard, and of course dogs like her are the living personification of this rule. These dogs will

stop at nothing to save a person or a relationship that needs saving. Florence once dragged her owners across a field and two orchards to save an injured cat that was too scared to climb down a plum tree. Now that's what I call friendship.

So even if you have just picked up this book in a shop or are browsing through a friend's copy and will remember nothing else, please remember this:

> Saving or improving just one relationship will make your life better; improving all of your relationships will utterly transform your whole life.

@COLLEGE

Start today by improving just one relationship and then repeat every day for the rest of your life. Life is too short for grudges and arguments.

@HOME

A home run along the lines of the Think Dog Rules will be a happy one. Share your copy of *Think Dog* with the rest of your family and create your own family charter based around the dog rules.

@WORK

Work by the dog rules and enjoy the career you deserve.

Help turn your workplace into a hive of great relationships and then watch it grow and grow.

FLORENCE THE ST BERNARD

Well, what can I say about Florence? She's fabulous! A giant in our pack, she is probably one of my most reliable and caring friends, and she is a real hit with humans when she lopes across the park. Children adore her and she adores them. Watch out for her slobber, though – when she shakes her head you need an umbrella!

STRIPPED TO THE BONE: CHUNK 4

Now you have read and understood Chunk 4 you should consider yourself fully house trained and ready to be let loose on the world.

- ❧ **It takes courage** – being a true friend involves making tough calls and personal sacrifices on occasion.
- ❧ **Lead the pack by example** – people listen to what you do, not what you say.
- ❧ **Give a dog a good name** – when you encourage someone it enhances and reflects well on everyone involved.
- ❧ **Handle criticism carefully** – constructive criticism is an essential part of being a friend and helping people grow.

- ❧ **Be your own dog** – you are a unique one-off: don't try to be something or someone you're not.
- ❧ **Every saved relationship enhances *you*** – saving even one relationship will enhance your life beyond measure.

LEARNING AND SHARING THE THINK DOG RULES

So there you have it, my 24 rules for life as tested by me and my doggy chums. Thinking like a dog can help almost anyone; anytime, anyplace, anywhere.

You will have seen the sections at the end of each rule where I have shown examples of how the rules can help in different situations – at school, at home and at work.

But that is just the beginning: here are some more examples of what you can do with the Think Dog Rules for Life.

@COLLEGE

Besides helping you as an individual, the Think Dog Rules for Life can be used in lots of other ways at school and at college.

One example is through drawing up a 'Think Dog Behaviour Contract'. These days the formation of a behavioural contract between pupils and teachers is a fun way to approach a serious subject. Use the Think Dog Rules, use the dog characters, make it interactive, get everyone involved and – most of all – stick to it.

These contracts are particularly appropriate for situations where children are joining a new secondary school, or the upper echelons of primary school.

At the other end of the spectrum, for college and school leavers, there is a massive opportunity to apply the Think Dog Rules in a business context. So much of the workplace today is dominated by relationships and yet so little is done to prepare young people to get the most out of them.

The Think Dog Rules for Life can form the basis of business awareness courses, training on the importance of relationships in the work environment and how to get the most out of work opportunities. Visit www.thinkdog.net to find out more.

@HOME

It is so easy to let relationships slip at home without even noticing it. The development of a family charter can pull the whole family together in the spirit of fun and cooperation. Using the Think Dog Rules for Life in everyday family situations can make a huge difference; if you would like to learn more about how they can help or find out about personal development courses then visit www.thinkdog.net

Will and Annalese specialise in working with family businesses to create 'Family Charters'; if you would like to find out more about these then visit www.familyfirms.net

@WORK

The opportunities for applying the Think Dog Rules for Life at work are endless as almost every problem in the workplace seems to boil down, to some extend at least, to poor relationships and communication.

Imagine *Think Dog* personal development training for new starters, or as a way of motivating and inspiring your organisation while injecting appropriate new behaviours into your corporate culture.

Consider the power of running imaginative sales training courses based on the Think Dog Rules for Life for your sales teams.

Think about the impact a presentation built around the Think Dog Rules for Life – complete with doggy anecdotes, animated stories and even occasional barking – could have on your next customer event, sales conference or company event.

If you would you like to see stronger leadership, more committed managers (your pack), improved staff loyalty and greater customer satisfaction, **then contact us.**

For more information about our Think Dog Rules for Life training programmes and presentations please visit:

❧ www.thinkdog.net

If you would like to know more about the help and support that Will and Annalese provide for businesses generally, please visit:

❧ www.murraymurray.com

ABOUT US

Think Dog Rules for Life is a working collaboration between Will Murray, Annalese Murray and their good friend Dog!

Life coaches and relationship troubleshooters with a difference, Will and Annalese have been helping people develop business and life-changing relationship skills for many years.

Cofounders of business relationship specialists Murray Murray (www.murraymurray.com) and family coaching business Family Firms (www.familyfirms.net), they work with all sorts of organisations and help people from all walks of life – from teachers to chairmen and students to lords and ladies.

Clients include the likes of:

* Orange, Fujitsu, British Energy, Glaxo Smith Kline and RWE nPower;
* Government agencies like the British Education Communication and Technology Agency (BECTA) and Sector Skills Councils;
* various trusts, charities, education institutions and schools;
* family businesses and private individuals.

Helping such a wide range of people overcome a whole host of different relationship problems is what has prompted them to collaborate on *Think Dog*.

But the real driving force behind the team is 'Dog' himself.

Despite never having done a proper day's work in his life, or maybe because of it, 'Dog' is a natural in the art of being everyone's best friend, and in getting the most out of life and those around him.

An expert in the art of both dog watching and people watching, it is his pearls of doggy wisdom that make *Think Dog* the life changer it is.

THINK DOG
HOW TO BE THE BEST

Will and Annalese Murray

Simple, straightforward and suitable for anyone from six to one hundred, *How to Be the Best* does exactly what it says on the cover: it tells you how to become the very best you can be.

Written by a bunch of wise, insightful dogs and two amazingly smart cats, it doesn't matter whether you are on your own individual mission, a family group with a big idea, a team with a challenge or even a whole organisation with an exciting new vision, this book will help you become the best at whatever you want to be.

Find out how developing a clear direction will help you:

- ❤ Focus on your critical priorities
- ❤ Build invaluable relationships
- ❤ Communicate in an amazingly appealing way
- ❤ Attract the most talented people to your cause
- ❤ Help you become the best there is!

For more information on *How to Be the Best* visit www.thinkdog.net